# WORK STYLE

*of the*

# ISTJ

Based on the Myers-Briggs Type Indicator®

# ANNE DRANITSARIS, PH.D.

Dranitsaris, Anne, 1949 –

## Work Style of the ISTJ

Includes bibliographical references and index.

ISBN 9781549957208

1. Myers-Briggs Type Indicator. 2. Psychology, Industrial. I. Title.

HF5548.8D72 2000        158.7
    C99-933107-8

Copyright 2017 Sage, Kahuna Enterprises Inc.

All rights reserved. No part of this book, except as specifically noted below, may be reproduced in any form or by any electronic or mechanical means including information storage and retrieval systems without permission in writing from the publisher. Exception: A reviewer may quote brief passages in a review.

Published by
Sage, Kahuna Enterprises
422 – 283 Danforth Ave
Toronto, ON M4K 1Y2

416.406.3939
www.AnneDranitsaris.com
www.StrivingStyles.com
www.WhoAreYouMeantToBe.com

Myers-Briggs Type Indicator and MBTI are registered trademarks of Consulting Psychologists Press, Inc., Palo Alto, CA

Printed in Canada

# Table of Contents

## Introduction

Introduction ................................................................... 1
What is the Myers-Briggs Type Indicator? ........................... 4
Your MBTI Test Results ................................................... 7

## General Information on Type

Preferences, Functions, and Attitudes ................................ 9
General Descriptions of the Sixteen Types ......................... 12
Using Personality Type at Work ...................................... 17

## Profile for the ISTJ

Primary Characteristics ................................................. 19
Communication Style ................................................... 25
Relationship Style ....................................................... 27
Learning Style ............................................................ 31
Career ..................................................................... 33
Employee Characteristics .............................................. 41
Team Contributions ..................................................... 48
Leadership Style ......................................................... 50

## Stress and Self-Protective Behavior

Stress and Self-Protective Behavior .................................. 53
Pressing the ISTJs Buttons ............................................ 58
Shifting from Self-Protective Behavior .............................. 59

## References

Bibliography .............................................................. 60
Anne Dranitsaris, Ph.D. ................................................ 62
Striving Styles & MBTI Services ...................................... 66
Striving Styles & MBTI Products ..................................... 69

# Work Style of the ISTJ

## Introduction

The Work Style Series was developed out of my own desire to have a comprehensive book on each personality type. There are many excellent books available that offer a small amount of information on the sixteen types, and individual booklets with a little information on the one type. However, not having access to all the information in one place constantly frustrated me, especially as I saw the need for it while working with organizational, team, and leadership development.

What I was really looking for was a personal reference book or "how to use" manual about each personality type for understanding their personality, along with the type of career, relationship, work and leadership style they have. This can be used for personal or professional development.

Each of the sixteen books in this series offers insight into how people of each personality type behave in the workplace. This offers individuals the opportunity to get to know all about work preferences. When used as a complete series, it provides a comprehensive reference on all types that is extremely helpful in an organizational or training context.

Using type in the workplace is most effective when you understand all the sixteen types. Knowledge of type will help improve your personal and professional relationships; it will help you focus on your own unique abilities and create the kind of work style that is best suited to the personality of your organization. Coming from a thorough knowledge of yourself, you are more able to explain your approach to work and can participate in creating a work environment that best suits your style.

I hope you will be able to use this book in the way in which it has been designed. This means that you will use it repeatedly. Read it

# WORK STYLE OF THE ISTJ

when you need direction. Read it when you need to explain yourself to someone. Read it when you recognize someone's frustration when working with you. Let others who you work with read it so they can understand your approach to work. It is not meant to be read once then put away. Like any other reference book, use it when you need to refer to something about yourself that you do not understand.

The common thread of typology is that there are many ways of being "normal" according to your individual personality type. Knowledge of typology lets understanding replace judgement and criticism, creating more productive and fulfilling relationships and workplaces. I have found using the Personality Profiles to be of enormous benefit to clients within my work in organizations and in my psychotherapy practice. It is my belief that it can provide you with a mechanism for developing your strengths, exercising your less developed functions, and letting others know about you, how to manage you, and what you need to perform optimally. I hope that the information in this book helps you fulfill your potential while bringing understanding and harmony to your working relationships with others.

The Work Style books have been designed as a practical guide to aid people at any level in an organization to better understand themselves and those with whom they work. People in work environments who use typology as a systematic, workable, logical tool for individual and organizational development become more efficient, productive, and, ultimately, financially successful.

By gaining an understanding of the theory and practice of typology, individuals become more familiar with their own personality and the personality types of others, and gain insight into why people act and react the way they do. As this happens, an appreciation of the differences in others and the unique abilities that each personality has begins to grow. Ultimately, this leads to a more harmonious and productive work environment.

# WORK STYLE OF THE ISTJ

The theory and practice of typology has its roots in the lifelong work of highly regarded researchers and practitioners such as Carl Gustav Jung, Isabel Myers, Katherine Briggs, and David Keirsey. The use of typology has grown over the years due to the contributions of these researchers, several other individuals, and their practices, teachings, and compilations of enormous amounts of research and statistics. Because of this, typology stands apart from many current theories about management effectiveness, team building, and how to motivate employees.

Although personality typing has been studied and variously described for hundreds of years, it was only during the first quarter of the 20th century that an accurate system to describe human behaviour evolved.

## Carl Gustav Jung

Psychological type is a theory of personality developed by Swiss psychiatrist Carl Jung to explain the innate differences in the behaviors, choices and forms of expression in healthy people. Unlike many of his contemporaries, Jung not only investigated psychological disorders or mental illness, but attempted to determine the basis for healthy psychological order in the human psyche. Jung inferred that people operate from different psychological frameworks and orientations, which are identifiable through observation and that we have physiological, inborn preferences for processing our experiences and interacting with the world.

Jung opened new ways of thinking about people and the behaviors with which people would respond in normal circumstances. He described behavioral predictability and provided a way to make reasonable assessments about people's differences in ideas, responses, and behaviors. He theorized that we have four different "functions" in our consciousness, and that the four functions are on two polar scales; two functions for "perceiving" (or gathering information), and two functions for "judging" (or making decisions).

# WORK STYLE OF THE ISTJ

Jung also believed that individuals prefer using one of the functions on each of the scales, and that it seemed like one of these two functions will be favored the most. He also theorized that people used these functions in either an extraverted or outwardly-directed fashion, or an introverted or inwardly directed fashion. He referred to the directional aspect as "attitudes in consciousness." Based on this model, Jung defined eight different functional patterns of behavior, or "types" with predictable patterns of behavior.

Jung described the behaviors and motivations of these eight different functions in his book, Psychological Types (1921), through characterizations of people who habitually prefer one pattern over another – his "eight types." Jung's theory of psychological types attempts to categorize people in terms of their primary modes of psychological/mental functioning, if we all have different functions and attitudes of consciousness.

## Katherine Briggs and Isabel Myers

The MBTI was the first effective tool for sorting the eight Jungian functions into the most to least favorite. It was created by Isabel Briggs-Myers and her mother, Katherine Briggs in the early 1940s to make Jung's theory useful for a more mainstream audience.

The original focus of the assessment was careers, as Briggs tried to help people select occupations that were best suited to their personality types during and following WWII. She believed this would help them lead healthier, happier lives.

## What is the Myers-Briggs Type Indicator?

Myers and Briggs created the MBTI based on four dichotomous scales, adding two new scales - Extroversion/Introversion and Judging/Perceiving - to Jung's original two function scales (judging functions: Thinking and Feeling, and perceiving functions: Intuition and Sensing) to make their psychometric instrument work.

# WORK STYLE OF THE ISTJ

As well, they replaced psychological type with personality type to make it palatable to people of that time. The MBTI soon found its place in organizations, because unlike Jung's theory, it did not discuss emotions or mental dysfunctions, or use other psychological words that would cause it to be rejected.

In the MBTI language, there are four dichotomous scales rather than the two that Jung identified. This differed from Jung's language, which identified the attitude the function operated in, and the mental process of the function. While Jung identified 8 psychological types, the MBTI identifies 16 personality types.

Myers and Briggs, the authors of the test, was determined to make Jung's Psychological Type theory useable in daily life. To do this, they departed from Jung in some significant ways. Jung's Theory incorporated the notion of development and individuation, however, the MBTI did not. It is solely a psychometric instrument.

The body of research and writing that gives credibility to the MBTI is based on the ongoing contributions of psychologists, consultants, coaches, trainers and facilitators who have integrated it into training and development programs, counseling, career counseling, leadership, team and employee development, culture, etc. The success of the application of the results of the MBTI is dependent upon their programs.

## Benefits of the MBTI

In general, the MBTI is a tool that helps people to:

- understand themselves and their behaviours.
- appreciate others and make constructive use of individual differences.

# WORK STYLE OF THE ISTJ

- see how approaching problems in different ways is healthy and productive for an organization.
- communicate more effectively with supervisors, peers, and employees.
- solve organizational or personal problems.
- make the most of the organization's human resources.
- assist in career choice and professional development.
- improve teamwork.
- understand and adapt to differences in management styles.
- understand contributions to the organization.
- understand some underlying causes of conflict.

For you to make the most of your results, it is important to understand that the MBTI

- describes behaviours rather than prescribes them.
- provides information about the preferences you indicated when answering the questionnaire.
- describes preferences, not skills, abilities, or intelligence.
- says that all preferences are equally important.
- has an organization devoted to continued research and development.
- does not seek to pigeon-hole people or put them into boxes.

# WORK STYLE OF THE ISTJ

## Who Uses the MBTI?

The MBTI has been employed as a tool for many years by a variety of users in small businesses and large corporations, service industries and manufacturing, consulting and training services, established firms and entrepreneurial ventures, and educational and health care institutions. The following offer some ideas about the versatility of the instrument based on its widespread application.

- Organizations in business, government, industry, and the military use it to understand communication, motivation, team building, career development, organization development, leadership development, and placement.

- Therapists and counsellors use the MBTI with individuals, couples, families, and groups for individual understanding and improving communication. It is also used in counselling for career change and exploration, marriage and couples counselling, student advising, conflict resolution, and personal growth.

- Educators at all levels use it to understand teaching and learning styles, aptitude, achievement, and motivation. It is extremely helpful in identifying learning styles, analyzing and improving curriculum, and in building relationships between teachers, administrators, and students.

- Spiritual groups of many denominations that are interested in individual differences in ministry and spirituality use the MBTI for individual, marriage, and couples counselling.

## Your MBTI Test Results

An individual's type is the combination of one preference from each of the four scales. Type is determined by the four preferences that were chosen when answering the questions on the MBTI.

# WORK STYLE OF THE ISTJ

A four-letter code is used as shorthand for indicating type. A letter (E, I, S, N, T, F, J, or P) represents each of the eight preferences. For example, ESTJ indicates a person who is energized by the external world (E), whose preferred way of attending to incoming information is sensing (S), whose way of deciding is thinking (T), and who adopts a judging (J) style of living. An individual's type is designated by this four-letter code, which indicates the individual's preference in each area.

The following pages provide information about what each of the four pairs of opposites means.

# Work Style of the ISTJ

## General Information on Personality Type

### Preferences, Functions, and Attitudes

According to psychological type theory, we are born with a predisposition for the functions and attitudes (orientation to the world) that we will prefer to use, and how we will like to use them. We have four pairs of opposing attitudes and functions in total, and we will prefer one from each group. Because we prefer them, we will use them more often and more naturally. They are more accessible to us and comfortable to use. Over time, we tend to rely on these functions and attitudes and, as a result, they become stronger and more developed as we progress in life.

Although our preferences come more easily, it does not mean that we cannot use and develop our other functions and attitudes when the situation demands. It means that it will take more energy and concentration to use them and we will not have as much dexterity and skill when we do.

Psychological preference does not represent an either/or concept. We can write with both hands, but prefer to use one above the other. It is important to remember that our preferences are dynamic and fluid, not cast in concrete. They relate to our selected way of behaving in most situations. All possible combinations of the functions and attitudes result in sixteen distinct personality types.

The following are brief descripts of the 4 functions along with information about their orientation and attitudes the functions are used in. Introversion and extraversion refer to the attitude the function is used in and Judging and perceiving relate to the orientation our function takes.

# WORK STYLE OF THE ISTJ

## Information Gathering Functions
## Sensing (S) and Intuition (N)

There are two ways we collect information. Sensing relates to the preference for paying attention to information that is perceived directly through the five senses, and for focusing on what actually exists. Intuition refers to the preference for paying attention to information that is taken in through a "sixth sense," and for noticing what might or could be rather than what actually exists.

## Deciding Functions
## Thinking (T) and Feeling (F)

There are two ways we make decisions. Thinking is the preference that relates to organizing and structuring information to decide in a logical and objective way. Feeling is related to the preference for organizing and structuring information to decide in a personal, subjective, values-oriented way.

## Attitudes of the Functions
## Extraversion (E) and Introversion (I)

These are the two ways a function can be energized. By extraverting it (using it and drawing energy from the external world of people, activities, and things) or by introverting it (using it and drawing energy from one's inner world of ideas, emotions, and impressions.) We either introvert or extravert a function and no one is a completely one way or another. We have four functions we most like to use and we introvert two and extravert the other two.

## Orientation of the Functions
## Judging (J) and Perceiving (P)

Judging and perceiving functions indicate whether the function is used for information gathering or for deciding. The orientation of our

## WORK STYLE OF THE ISTJ

predominant function impacts how we organize or don't organize our lives. We use our judging functions to decide and these functions (Thinking & Feeling) relates to living a decided, planned and organized life, while our perceiving functions (Intuition & Sensing) refers to the preference for living in a more spontaneous and flexible way.

# WORK STYLE OF THE ISTJ

## General Descriptions of the Sixteen Types

**ESTJ**

"Take-charge" people. Well-organized, disciplined, and dependable, they are often found in leadership roles. Have a definite need to be in control. Generally outgoing, take responsibilities, but not themselves, seriously. Prefer being among people; team players, work best with plans and lists, impatient with theory or abstractions. Can be autocratic and demanding of others.

**ENTJ**

Believe they were born to lead. Desire to take charge and organize those around them. Well-informed, decisive, accumulate knowledge. May be more positive and confident than experience warrants. Global perspective, see things long-range, tough when appropriate. Great strategists and builders of organizations. Can be arrogant, critical, and intimidating. High expectations for themselves and others.

**INTP**

"Human computers" who possess an amazing capacity for storing information. Enjoy theoretical or scientific subjects; high need for clarity. Use hair-splitting logic and analysis. Fiercely independent, perfectionistic, theoretical, self-sufficient, precise in thought and language, have technological curiosity, lose sense of time and space. Distant except with close friends. Need time alone for best work. Not impressed by authority.

**ISTP**

Action-oriented with an insatiable curiosity and a need to know what makes things "tick." Often technically gifted, they are interested in facts and practicality. Make judgements based on facts, not values. Not naturally in-tune with people's feelings or emotions. Operate best when they are on their own. Use as little energy as possible to accomplish a task.

## ENFP

Powerful persuaders with an abundance of charm, warmth, and ingenuity. Quick with solutions, ready to help anyone with a problem. Great improvisers who can neglect detail and facts. Rationalize wants and needs. People-pleasers, give and seek affirmation, intensely involved, have insight into the potential of others. Impulsive and easily bored, always looking for more exciting possibilities. Correct perceptions can lead to wrong conclusions.

## ENTP

Highly energetic, alert, charming, and enthusiastic. Enjoy arguing for the competitive fun of it. Resourceful problem solvers. Seek to understand people; perceptive, future-oriented, excited about pursuing new ideas. Great persuaders; at times forceful. Tend to dominate others without always being aware. Not detail-oriented and unimpressed by authority. Get by with brilliance, a flair for the dramatic – and by the skin of their teeth.

## INTJ

High achievers with powerful personalities. Go after the goals they set for themselves with a vengeance. Sceptical, critical, independent, determined, often stubborn. Intellectually creative with great confidence in their insights. Single-minded and tenacious, tend to go to extremes. Analytical and theoretical, drive selves and others equally hard. Unimpressed with authority, large privacy needs.

# WORK STYLE OF THE ISTJ

## INFJ

Gentle and gracious, yet distant. Willing to share themselves but only on their own terms. Firm principles and values. Highly insightful and intuitive, have trouble dealing with conflict. Dislike insincerity. Prone to bursts of stubbornness; idealistic, slow to state needs, reserved, quietly forceful. Success achieved through perseverance. Excellent organizational skills.

## ESFJ

True "people" people. Put others at ease with their genuine warmth and generosity. Always doing something nice for someone. Have a high need for affirmation and approval. Possess a strong sense of responsibility and high regard for authority. Little interest in abstract thinking or technical subjects. Mainly interested in things that visibly affect people's lives.

## ENFJ

Responsive and responsible, they have a gift for seeing human potential. Outgoing and charismatic, they make wonderful speakers. Responsive to praise and criticism. Have a great deal of compassion for others. Insightful, sensitive to indifference, natural and credible leaders, ministers. Tend to idealize relationships; take conflict and rejection personally. Own needs can sometimes be overlooked or ignored.

## INFP

Shy, private, yet people-oriented. Focus on human potential and improving the world. Friendly, often absorbed in what they are doing. Put great importance on values, idealistic to a cause or leader. Desires harmony; compassionate, quietly stubborn, self-critical, sensitive. Closed down by too much structure or rules. Tend to set extremely high standards for themselves. Perfectionists who often undervalue themselves.

# WORK STYLE OF THE ISTJ

## ISFP

Outwardly carefree and light-hearted but driven by deeply held values. Hands-on problem solvers who are extraordinarily empathetic. Penetratingly accurate in their judgements of others. Can be hampered by their deep desire to please. Intensely practical, they live in the here-and-now – not in a hurry to move along. Not interested in leading despite often having a loyal following.

## ESTP

Outgoing, straight-shooters with a flair for the dramatic. Quick to size-up a situation and act on their assessment. Do not mince words and can be somewhat insensitive. Bend rules and regulations to fit their needs. Usually willing to sacrifice their position before doing something they know is wrong. Live in the here-and-now; best when treating life as an adventure.

## ESFP

Outgoing, friendly, sociable. They are natural performers with an innate ability for sports. Tend to keep their judgements of others to themselves. Keenly aware of what is going on and join in eagerly. Find remembering facts easier than mastering theories. Don't mind chaos but can be too impulsive. Are best in situations that need sound common sense and practical ability.

## ISTJ

Private with a distinct need for personal distance. Great organizers who take life seriously and possess a great sense of responsibility and dependability. Keenly aware of laws, traditions, and regulations, and expect others to abide by them. Steadfastly work toward goals unaware or in spite of any negative impact it may have on others. Achieve success through perseverance.

# WORK STYLE OF THE ISTJ

**ISFJ**

Excel at followership. Love to help others and attend to their physical needs. View the world in literal and practical terms. Extraordinarily sensitive to others' feelings; they are generous, warm, caring. Painstakingly thorough and detail-oriented. Can be hard on themselves and may suffer from low self-esteem. Most likely to sacrifice for others or for the job or project.

# Work Style of the ISTJ

## *Using Personality Type at Work*

Within organizations, understanding and applying the theory and practice of personality type can profoundly affect people and the overall work environment and culture. As it is normal and healthy for people working together to have a variety of opinions and attitudes, the challenge facing leaders is how to direct these distinct personalities so they work effectively toward a common vision with synergy and group cohesiveness.

Human motivation comes from within each individual, and no leader, regardless of how effective he or she is, can motivate people unless they choose to be motivated. Exceptional performance by ordinary people occurs when leaders have worked with their people from the "inside out" rather than from the "outside in." Effective leaders work with their employees to develop and maximize employees' potential and do not waste time and negative energy trying to make people fit a specific mould or perform a certain way.

Using typology, a leader can learn to understand what motivates each individual and then create the conditions for superior performance. Typology can assist in developing a culture that is creative, productive, and fulfills both personal and organizational goals.

As an individual within a company, each person can be aided by typology to better understand how he or she prefers to function in everyday working situations. As individuals begin to comprehend their own preferences and the forces that direct them, they gain a better appreciation of their own styles and unique abilities. It will also become increasingly evident that other people are quite different in their styles and abilities. They are motivated by different things and have their own distinct reactions to change, stress, and challenges.

By adopting this approach to working with others, individuals will more readily accept and understand others from their own frame of reference, building bridges between the gaps that naturally occur between types, positively effecting communication, teamwork, and interpersonal relationships. It will help leaders to build on their employees' strengths rather than struggle with their weaknesses.

# WORK STYLE OF THE ISTJ

## Primary Characteristics of the ISTJ

*Dominant Function:* Introverted Sensing
*Auxiliary Function:* Extraverted Thinking
*Tertiary Function:* Introverted Feeling
*Inferior Function:* Extraverted Intuition

**Approximately 11.6% of the general population are ISTJs.**

ISTJs are serious, responsible, and sensible, often characterized as pillars of society. They are noticeably the most reliable of all sixteen types and are driven by their sense of responsibility and duty. You can always trust ISTJs, for their word is their solemn vow.

As the major themes of ISTJs are responsibility, duty, and doing what one should do, they have a very strong set of rules and principles that govern their lives, and the lives of those over whom they have influence. They are cautious and traditional in all they say and do, and like things to be said in a factual, no-frills manner. They say what they mean and mean what they say.

### Still waters run deep...

ISTJs approach the outer world with a cool, impersonal, and aloof manner, while inside themselves they are storing detailed impressions of what they are experiencing. Experiences form structural guidelines for ISTJs, who can later recall these experiences when a similar situation presents itself and use them to guide their responses and behaviour. ISTJs see and remember everything in detail and relate it to what they feel is meaningful.

ISTJs will appear calm in a crisis. They may have very strong reactions yet will maintain a quiet, persevering approach to the problem, with a clear focus and willingness to stand their ground and do what has to be done.

# Work Style of the ISTJ

Their perseverance tends to stabilize everything with which they are involved. They are thorough, extremely patient with details, and will keep working at something long after others have given up. They will take on the work of others rather than leave important tasks undone. They will not quit unless experience tells them they are wrong.

## Facts, details, experiences...

ISTJs have an exceptional facility and talent for working with details and facts. They are like storage vaults for accumulated information about all kinds of impersonal data they can recall at will. This computer-like faculty is internal, so they are best able to access information and make connections between details when they are alone. This brings them to a further understanding of their duties and commitments and allows them time to organize their external world so they can successfully complete their tasks and responsibilities. ISTJs do not share this information freely with others and quite often must be pushed or probed to get anything more from them than a bottom-line decision or action plan.

ISTJs also use this proficiency with data to support their view of things. They call upon past experiences to help them while in the process of making new decisions. They tend to think inductively, using their data to define and solve their problems. ISTJs do not allow themselves to make impulsive decisions, and approach their tasks in an organized and systematic way. They follow policies and procedures and do not have time for people who do not. Change is never made for the sake of change itself.

One of the greatest strengths of ISTJs is their ability to trust their experience and vast collection of facts. This helps ISTJs respond to situations in life in a way that uses their experience well. However, if they have had few experiences, their ability to respond to new challenges will be equally limited. If their experience has been wide and varied, they are able to respond with much more versatility. They

# Work Style of the ISTJ

run the risk of becoming narrow and inflexible if they do not broaden life experiences or do not have an eclectic group of friends from whose experiences they can draw. For ISTJs to develop to their full capacity, they need to break away from their tried and true way of operating.

## Talented organizers with innate work ethic...

ISTJs go through life learning what is necessary to do and then doing it in a logical, practical, and organized manner. They are extremely hard workers and are often found in managerial positions because they can be trusted to accomplish whatever they set out to do in an orderly fashion. Once they commit to something they are unstoppable, and will work long and hard to meet their objectives using a practical and common-sense approach.

To meet their need for certainty, ISTJs set up and enjoy order and routines. They need to know what is coming next is the same as what came before. This ensures feeling stable and secure. ISTJs have rules for everything in their lives, as rules provide them with clear direction and limits. Rules enable them to know what they can and cannot do, and, therefore, minimize any potential errors. ISTJs usually organize every aspect of their lives down to the smallest detail. They have difficulty being objective about this exceptional talent for organization and are sure they could be better at it.

## Do not trust things they have no experience with...

ISTJs trust the information their senses provide them and little else. Often, they have a sceptical and critical attitude toward new information with which they have had no experience. They do not easily trust people who are careless with facts and details. Solid facts are preferred over imagination and possibilities. They are not comfortable when they have to take a leap of faith or move beyond their realm of experience. They need time to thoroughly absorb and understand something before they can move ahead.

# Work Style of the ISTJ

Preparing for an unknown future by living frugally and taking care of their financial future comes easily to ISTJs. They enjoy reviewing and revising existing systems to improve cost effectiveness and to maximize efficiency. Known for their economic natures, they are very much aware of the value of money. They carefully weigh all features and benefits before making a major purchase and are adept at handling their own and other people's money.

ISTJs take nothing for granted and assume nothing. They concentrate on what is objective, immediate, and concrete. They can focus absolutely on doing what needs to be done, in the moment, to the exclusion of everything else. However, they also expect others to behave in the same way, which can make ISTJs seem excessively demanding. ISTJs can be easily stereotyped as a classic type A personality – driven, obsessive, and impatient.

# Work Style of the ISTJ

## Communication Style of the ISTJ

With their efficiency orientation, ISTJs communicate in a practical and factual manner. They are easy to recognize since they often don't speak until spoken to, and when they do, they use as few words as possible. They are cautious and brief in all they say and do, and like things to be said in a factual, no-frills manner. They say what they mean, and mean what they say. They would rather do something than talk about it, although they can be counted on for their cautious, sometimes pessimistic attitude: they enjoy pointing out what is wrong with the world, whether it's healthcare, politicians or teachers. They are quick to express their judgments without thinking of the impact this has on others.

ISTJs communicate with others on a need-to-know basis. They are extremely self-contained and will often withhold information. Their low need for self-expression and high need for privacy can cause others around them to have difficulty knowing what they feel or even understanding what is going on with the ISTJ. If you ask, they may tell you, but sometimes you have to pry things out of them.

Too often, to the frustration of others, ISTJs need to be pushed or probed before they will offer anything more than a look, a judgment or a question about what you want from them. Many people believe that the ISTJ doesn't like them or is angry with them, since they rarely ask questions about what is happening in the lives of other people. ISTJs can be shocked to find out that people are affected by their behavior, because to them, they are showing how much they care by working as hard as they do.

ISTJs rely on logic and order to help them maintain a sense of security and predictability. They do not find emotional expression useful, and they feel very unsafe when others expect them to share personal information about themselves. They prefer everyone to communicate in the same logical and unemotional way that they do.

# WORK STYLE OF THE ISTJ

They feel awkward in situations that call for them to express any emotions, even appreciation or gratitude. Interpersonal interactions cause them a great deal of anxiety, since there is no prescribed outcome, and logic doesn't always apply. Their uncommunicative attitude can sometimes create very serious interpersonal problems in relationships and at work. ISTJs figure if someone wants them to know, they will tell them.

## Private and self-contained...

ISTJ do not pay much attention to their emotions and rarely share what they feel with others. They are intensely private people. They have difficulty connecting to people on a relational level, even those they have been friends with for years. Conversations focus on facts and information they feel others need to know. They do not spend time talking about their feeling, dreams or hopes for the future.

As they are realistic and practical people, they have trouble relating to others who are open with their visions and ideas. If they cannot see the usefulness in an idea, they are quick to judge it as impractical and dismiss the conversation. Because of their lack of emotional sensitivity, they can unintentionally discourage others from sharing their thoughts and ideas.

The ISTJ does not know how to respond to someone seeking deep and meaningful conversation. They simply prefer exchange of information to be of a practical and useful nature, and any other conversation makes them feel anxious and inadequate. They make sure to keep themselves busy to avoid this type of conversation with their partner.

# Work Style of the ISTJ

## Relationships with the ISTJ

ISTJs are self-controlled, well disciplined, and dedicated to preserving traditional values and time-honoured institutions. They have a strong sense of family and community responsibility and show their commitment by bringing order and structure into the lives of others.

Because of their need for certainty and security, ISTJs take their personal relationships very seriously. Although their work comes first, when that is done, they put time and effort into their family and recreational lives. Rules and regulations are freely imposed on family members and they expect to be followed without question or exception. Hierarchical in nature, ISTJs see themselves as being at the top of the chain of command. They deferred to their own parents in the past, and expect their children to do the same. The roles within the family are clearly defined, with each person having his or her own responsibilities.

ISTJs feel that leisure time must be earned. They will not leave work unfinished to go play unless circumstances support it or they feel their duty to the family or organization requires it. Often, they have to schedule time to relax because it does not come naturally to them. When relaxing, ISTJs will show a side of themselves not readily apparent in their duty-bound work life. They will say whatever comes to mind, which could be absurd, irrelevant, unpredictable, or even droll. This often catches others off-guard, since it is so unlike ISTJs to switch off duty long enough for others to enjoy this zanier side of them.

### Show caring through responsibility…

The way ISTJs show they care is through their strong sense of responsibility. They are extremely loyal to their workplace and the individuals with whom they work. They are intensely private people who rarely demonstrate to others what is going on underneath their calm exterior.

ISTJs usually master appropriate social graces and interpersonal skills because it is expected of them, rather than for their own personal reasons. They can appear extraverted if the situation or their job requires this type of behaviour. Meeting behavioural expectations often propels them into leadership positions in school, work, and the community. They will put their duties ahead of their own personal needs, wants, and likes.

## Need to be useful...

ISTJs show they care by protecting and serving the people in their lives. They have a low need to relate to others, but a high need to do things for them. Conservative and traditional by nature, they strive to uphold a sense of continuity in their families. They uphold family rituals, ceremonies, and traditions and maintain habits and attitudes passed down from generation to generation. They do not question why, nor do they spend time thinking about doing things differently as they do not consider it worth the effort.

These trustworthy, loyal and dependable people will do anything for their friends and employees. They can be counted on to do the things they say they will and to work tirelessly to honor their commitments. The way ISTJs show they care is through their strong sense of responsibility. Because of this, they can be used shamelessly by friends, family and co-workers, who automatically go to them for help during times of need. If someone has a job that needs doing – whether painting an apartment, cleaning the community center or getting a work project in on time – the ISTJ rarely will say no when asked for help. This happens in many of their relationships. Even if they do complain about all the demands made on them, they rarely want others to do anything about it. They may even protest if anyone tries to relieve them of what they believe is their responsibility.

# Work Style of the ISTJ

ISTJs are not naturally connected to their emotions. They are focused on helping others by doing what needs to be done and by being useful. They will keep themselves from connecting to their feelings by staying busy or by numbing them with alcohol or food. Although this keeps their inner sense of stability, it can lead to further problems down the road. They also have difficulty dealing with the emotions of others, and tend to avoid issues in their relationships by burying themselves in work.

## Strong sense of duty and tradition...

ISTJs are the calm, quiet pillars of the community, the "rock" of the family and the "go-to" person if you need a helping hand. They offer their quiet support in everything they do. Because of their introverted nature, they reveal themselves by what they produce and build --- whether it is financial security, a solid home in a good community, or the moral compass of their family. They have a calm forcefulness that encourages people to rally around them, easily depending on them for no other reason than that they feel so solid.

They take rules very seriously – whether they are rules imposed by society, by their parents, or by other authorities – because they see it as their duty to follow them. They are responsible people, who become anxious when others do not follow rules or meet their commitments. ISTJs follow social and legal rules, pay their taxes early, and volunteer their time to community events.

ISTJs will establish their close relationships with the intention of maintaining them for a lifetime. While slow to develop, relationships with a ISTJ are characterized by deep commitment and loyalty.

# Work Style of the ISTJ

## Learning Style

ISTJs learn best with subjects and methods that involve a step-by-step process which takes them through from beginning to end, with each step building on the last. Enjoying subjects that are practical and useful, ISTJs are tenacious and persevering with their studies. They trust and prefer concrete and useful information and have a very low tolerance for anything abstract or theoretical, especially if it does not lead to a specific end.

As students, ISTJs need their teachers to be precise and accurate if they are going to trust the information being taught. They also need their learning materials to be correct and can easily be side-tracked by typographical or grammatical errors, as these lead them to believe there could be larger mistakes. Reassurance is needed when this occurs.

ISTJs need their learning environment to be well structured and task-oriented, with clear, precise assignments and objective methods for marking and measuring performance. If they find the subject enjoyable or too easy, they can become sceptical of its value. They easily delineate between play and work, and since learning is work, it should not be easy or fun. ISTJs want their class to begin and end on time and have little tolerance or respect for others who do not agree with this thinking.

### Need well defined, step-by-step approaches...

ISTJs learn best with subjects that require memory work and recall, and utilize workbooks where they can see their steady progress. They also enjoy learning activities that provide time for them to think about what they have learned. They learn quickly if given specific examples and situations where they can observe, quantify, and measure the subject they are studying.

## Work Style of the ISTJ

ISTJs have difficulty with the learning process if they cannot master a step and are forced to move on before they are ready. They can easily give up on something, thinking they are like other types, who can jump ahead to conclusions before gathering all the information, when in fact they need all the facts before coming to a conclusion.

# Work Style of the ISTJ

## *Career*

ISTJs tend to establish a career path for themselves early in life and work tenaciously to arrive at their chosen goal through hard work and diligence. Their choices are often large, stable organizations where their security needs are met, providing them with the opportunity to prove themselves in their chosen field.

The professions that are attractive to ISTJs are those that offer practical and tangible results such as dentistry, accounting, and law. These professions involve set ways of doing things and frequently require working alone to achieve a specific result.

Any occupation that requires accuracy, attention to detail, and follow-through is attractive to ISTJs. They are more comfortable in work environments where the focus is on the production of a specific product, as they are not comfortable when required to interact spontaneously with a lot of people. They do not expect their work to meet their social needs, nor do they tend to form friendships on the job. Usually they choose a career where they can get ahead by learning the rules and adhering to them.

ISTJs are found in the upper levels of large and small organizations, in management positions and as executives. Decisive, logical, and analytical, they know how to run a tight ship. They tend to make exceptional lawyers, because they are so thorough in their inspection of details and data that it is rare anything slips by them. They make particularly fine contract and tax attorneys for this reason.

ISTJs tend to be serious and businesslike in all they do. Realistic in their assessment of their skills and what they are capable of, they rarely take on anything they consider beyond their capabilities. When ISTJs decide they can do something, it is because they can.

**The following occupations have been found to be most appealing to ISTJs:**

# Work Style of the ISTJ

## Business, Leadership and Professional Roles

ISTJs love business, and they are likely to be found at all levels of any organization. They have a natural ability to keep things on track – managing structures, systems and operations to keep businesses moving towards achieving their objectives. If considering a career in business, it will be important for the ISTJ to look for organizations that are more traditional in nature, where they can maintain or stabilize operations.

These types of organizations provide the ISTJ with many of the elements they need to be satisfied, including clearly defined roles, management of resources and standard operating procedures for every task. Their practical nature and detail-orientation makes them effective at attending to costs and the bottom line, following goals, paths, timelines and measuring and achieving results in a prescribed way. They are likely to prefer businesses that are involved with tangible products or services, rather than creative or intellectual property.

Because of the very strong work ethic, the ability to put aside personal priorities to achieve work and career goals, and the sheer capacity to just get work done, ISTJs are often found at the upper levels of both small and large organizations, in management and as executives. ISTJs may not even seek out leadership or management roles, but end up there through promotion. Their innate sense of responsibility and willingness to self-sacrifice for the sake of the greater good can lead them to take on roles managing or leading people that they don't even desire, because they see it as their duty to those who would promote them.

ISTJs naturally know how to run a tight ship, where there is order, where decisions are made logically and in a timely fashion, and where information is analyzed thoroughly to minimize risk before decisions

# Work Style of the ISTJ

are made. ISTJs are often effective in driving themselves and others to achieve the tangible goals of any organization they might work for.

ISTJs have tremendous powers of concentration and an ability to absorb and store in an orderly manner great amounts of factual data. Many careers in the legal field require these talents and, as they take nothing for granted and their critical minds are adept at catching factual oversights, ISTJs excel at these careers. ISTJs often make excellent lawyers, especially contract and tax attorneys, because of their thoroughness in inspecting details and data. Things rarely slip by them.

- Accountant / Actuary
- Auditor
- Chief Executive Office / Chief Operating Officer
- Chief Information Officer
- Efficiency Expert / Analyst
- Manager / Supervisor – Junior to Executive Levels
- Manager – Office / Logistics & Supply / Inventory / Operations
- Quality System / Regulatory Compliance Officer / Auditor
- Insurance Underwriter
- Lawyer / Attorney
- Logistics and Supply Manager
- Manager / Supervisor
- Office Manager
- Paralegal
- Regulatory Compliance Officer
- Word Processing Specialist

## Administrative

ISTJs tend to make excellent administrative and support staff. Their task-orientation and serious focus on their responsibilities means they will ensure the details of the work and business are attended to

## Work Style of the ISTJ

without exception and with high quality. ISTJs are likely to find satisfiers in many administrative fields – business administration, accounting, legal or financial institutions, for example. In the medical field, clinics or hospital administrative roles may be attractive to them as these are places they can create and maintain an orderly environment that is task-related and where operations are completed according to a specific schedule.

ISTJs will work best in support roles where they have detailed expectations for their role defined, where they are left to work independently to meet those expectations, and where tasks and responsibilities vary little from day to day.

- Office Administrator / Administrative Assistant
- Administrator – Educational / Personnel
- Administrator – Health Care / Medical Records
- Assistant – Medical / Dental / Legal
- Clerical Worker
- Computer Operator
- Bank Teller
- Paralegal / Court Clerk

### Sales and Service

ISTJs do well in service or sales industries where they can work with products or services that they have personal experience with, and where there are clearly defined methods and policies for interacting with clients. Field technical service is an example of this type of work, where they are given details of an issue, which they can trouble shoot and make repairs according "to the manual," then deal with people according to the defined company policy.

Sales careers or jobs where there is a pre-established customer is more desirable for ISTJs, as these would enable them to focus on servicing and selling where a relationship already exist, and prices are already set.

# Work Style of the ISTJ

ISTJs won't be great at negotiating on the spot, or reading the non-verbal cues people give through their body language, so they would do best where they have a specific sales procedure to follow. Having to do sales where the results are unpredictable, such as in cold calling or tele-sales, simply does not meet their need for security.

- Customer Service Representative
- Sales Representative – Retail / Industrial / Medical / Technical
- Inside Sales or Sales Support Representative
- Car Salesperson
- Service / Installation Representative – Information Services / Telephone / Cable
- Sports Equipment/Merchandise Sales
- Technical Support / Field Service

## Public Service

In the service industries ISTJs abound as they enjoy doing their duty by serving their community. Jobs in the civil service, police department, and careers where they can serve and protect people appeal to them. They do their best work within a well-structured environment with clear rules for behaviour, which these areas provide.

- Corrections Officer
- District Attorney
- Government Employee / Civil Servant
- Judge
- Meter Reader
- Military: Officer / Soldier
- Police Officer / Detective
- Politician
- Probation Officer

# Work Style of the ISTJ

- Security Guard
- Taxation Examiner / Agent /Auditor

## Finance

ISTJs are well suited towards a career in finance because of their natural detail-orientation and their affinity for working with the predictable nature of numbers. Careers in this field require a high degree of accuracy and precision, which ISTJs are known for and which they easily provide. Working in the areas of finance, where predetermined outcomes are expected, means a career involving a low degree of risk as well.

Another advantage is that these careers frequently require them to work alone with little distraction – ideal for the serious, results-oriented ISTJ.

- Accountant / Bookkeeper
- Actuary
- Banker / Bank Examiner
- Budget Analyst
- Chief Financial Officer
- Auditor – Internal/ Financial
- Analyst – Credit/ Budget
- Credit Analyst / Counsellor
- Estate Planner
- Credit Counselor
- Estate Planner
- Investment Securities Officer
- Stockbroker
- Tax Examiner

## Education

# WORK STYLE OF THE ISTJ

What better way to contribute to building a strong foundation in society than through the field of education? ISTJs will often be found working in elementary school where they get the opportunity to interact personally with students while teaching them basic skills and rules.

ISTJs may also find specialized educational areas appealing, because they can work with smaller groups with special needs. The area of educational administration may also be attractive to ISTJs, particularly where it allows them to have governance over a specific area, or where they can be in charge of maintaining the school operation and ensuring curriculum is followed.

ISTJs also enjoy teaching subjects that are technical and practical. Being able to give concrete information to their students in a hands-on style following specific criteria is very enjoyable for ISTJs. They are also drawn to careers in the administrative side of education where they are in charge of maintaining the operation of the school curriculum. They may also enjoy library sciences, where interaction with people is minimal, but there is plenty of opportunity to work independently, while structuring and handling vast amounts of information.

- Administrator
- High School Teacher – Science / Technical / Industrial / Math
- High School Teacher – Physical Education
- Librarian
- School Principal
- Preschool / Elementary School Teacher
- Religious Educator

## Health Care and Helping Professionals

Careers in the health care field can be very satisfying to ISTJs because they provide the opportunity to build a solid foundation of

## Work Style of the ISTJ

technical skills. There is a traditional aspect to these careers, where respect and authority is usually granted to them because of their professional title, and where they can service the greater good and well-being of their community in real and practical ways. These careers usually include structured procedures and protocols that guide their behavior and interactions. Within these practices, they can use their natural detail-orientation to gather facts of a patient's symptoms, draw specific conclusions, and offer prescribed advice or treatment programs.

Occupations such as dentistry or pharmacology also provide the opportunity to master information and skills, and then use them in the same way repeatedly. These professions provide skills that are useful and marketable anywhere they go, thus providing the ISTJ with lifelong security and employment.

- Biomedical Technologist
- Chiropractor
- Dentist / Dental Hygienist
- Dietician / Nutritionist
- Exercise Physiologist
- General Surgeon / Practitioner
- Health Care Administrator
- Home Health Aid
- Lab Technologist
- Medical Researcher
- Nurse / Nursing Administrator
- Optometrist / Optician
- Pharmacist / Pharmacy Technician
- Primary Care Physician
- Speech Pathologist
- Therapist: Massage / Physical
- Veterinarian

## Technical and Research

# Work Style of the ISTJ

Most technical fields and careers have very specific guidelines for accuracy, and emphasize adherence to codes and procedures. This eliminates ambiguity and risk – exactly what ISTJs prefer in the type of work they do. These fields require them to have specific training and acquired skills. The work is "hands-on" and typically, they see immediate, tangible results of their work.

In research fields, ISTJs will be able to use their ability to probe information intensely to obtain specific answers. Legal research, for example, utilizes these talents, plus their critical ability to spot factual errors, oversights and to take nothing for granted. Technical fields utilize these same skills, while giving them opportunity to work on their own. Technical fields also provide opportunities to work within specific structures and systems accurately while following set procedures

- Agricultural Scientist
- Computer Programmer
- EEG Technologist / Technician
- Genealogist
- Geologist
- Law Researcher
- Mine Surveyor
- Technical Writer
- Technologist/ Researcher – Medical/Biomedical
- Technician – Radiology / Lab

## Skilled Labor

These professions can be very enjoyable and provide many career satisfiers for an ISTJ. This type of work allows them to see the practical and tangible results of their hard work.

A career in one of these fields allows an ISTJ to develop their skills in a particular area and apply them in a repetitive way, eventually

## WORK STYLE OF THE ISTJ

reaching the level of mastery. They are able build their abilities from the ground up, and take on greater challenges incrementally to grow along the way at a slow yet steady pace. These occupations provide hands-on opportunities to use their problem-solving skills, their attention to detail, and their ability to follow work through to completion. The work will be particularly satisfying to the ISTJ it involves the production of a specific product.

- Carpenter
- Contractor / Handyman
- Electrician
- Glazier / Glass Fitter
- Machinist
- Mechanic – Airplane / Auto
- Painter
- Plumber
- Welder

Remember, these are only some areas that provide satisfying expression for the unique, natural talents of the ISTJ.

# Work Style of the ISTJ

## Work Style

This section provides an overview of how this personality type functions in the work environment. Understanding the natural abilities and proficiencies of each type, and providing individuals with the opportunity to express their abilities at work, allows employees to function optimally and contribute their best efforts to the team.

## The ISTJ Employee

The ISTJ employee is, above all else, dependable and responsible. ISTJs are driven by accountability, productivity, and the bottom line. They can be counted on to do the right thing for the right person at the right time. If they know the specific criteria for what they are supposed to deliver, they will act quickly and correctly. They have a tremendous capacity for following through and staying with projects until completion, and are usually the last ones at the office to leave, wanting every last detail to be dealt with before calling it a day.

### Responsible and reliable...

ISTJ employees are predictable in their approach to work. A stable environment is preferred, where they can attend to the tasks of their work in an orderly fashion. They generally need a fair amount of privacy and long stretches of uninterrupted time to do their best work.

ISTJs are extremely hard-working people. They enjoy responsibility and actively seek it out, holding themselves accountable for their commitments to others. They tend to disapprove of others who do not have this same work ethic.

# Work Style of the ISTJ

This type of worker can be relied upon to meet deadlines with little fanfare. Adherence to deadlines is imperative. When they commit themselves to completing a project on time, ISTJs will do whatever it takes to make sure they keep their word. They do not believe in skipping over things to meet a deadline. Doing things properly, thoroughly, and completely is their bottom line, and they expect that others will adhere to it as well.

Because they are stable and reliable, ISTJs are often given positions of responsibility within organizations. It is easy to depend upon them to be there because of their reliable nature. ISTJs prefer to work for and with other hard-working people who are focused on details and results. They are generally calm, cool, and collected even under great stress. Often perceived to be unfeeling by others, they tend not to demonstrate what is going on inside themselves. However, they are extremely effective in handling crises because they do not let their personal reactions get in the way, and simply set about doing what needs to be done to remedy the situation.

ISTJs are prone to taking on excessive amounts of responsibility. They can be depended upon to perform specific tasks when these are laid out for them in concrete ways. They can respond quite harshly when others do not act in the same way.

## Stability and strong work ethic...

The ISTJ employees' mandate is to fulfill their responsibilities, do their duties, and be productive, and they do not feel satisfied until this is done. For them, work comes before play; vacations are rewards for work accomplished and should not be taken until the work is done.

ISTJs prefer working for companies that provide a tangible service or product, where performance is measured in a structural and specific way with objective rewards. They believe their paycheque is reward enough for their work and is the only yardstick they use to measure how well they have done. They do not seek attention or crave the limelight, nor are they particularly free with their appreciation of others, except when performance has truly been above and beyond the call of duty.

This type of employee can be counted on for longevity. They like their lives to be stable, and they seek out stable organizations where they can put in their time, work hard, and retire with a gold watch. They are vulnerable to staying with a job they do not particularly enjoy maintaining financial and professional stability. ISTJs are willing to sacrifice a great deal to provide for their financial futures. They dislike having to depend on anyone so will work very hard to avoid being in this position.

Others often see ISTJs as obsessive. They work hard, play hard, and live by the bottom line. Steady and constant, they are willing to change only when they see a practical reason to do so. They are the solid, predictable workers who provide valuable stability and constancy in an organization.

## Value hierarchy, structure and tradition...

The chain of command is extremely important to the ISTJ. It provides them with the type of structure within which they are most productive. In fact, although ISTJs make up only 9% of the general population in the United States, they comprise approximately 30% of the US Armed Forces.

To ISTJs, structure and systems equal security. They have difficulty when required to go along with someone else's plans or ideas without first having all the details, specifics, and quantifiable outcomes.

Being stability-oriented, ISTJs work diligently to preserve the structure of the organization through adherence to standard operating procedures. They will cooperate as long as things are done by the book. Anyone not conforming will quickly be admonished for his or

## Work Style of the ISTJ

her behaviour and will be a focus for the ISTJ until the deviant behaviour is corrected.

Authority is given by ISTJs to those in positions of power. Because of this, they do not concern themselves as much with the reason for a policy as they do with who has the authority to implement it. They do not invite or welcome challenges to established authority. Because of their strong orientation toward authority based on chain of command, ISTJs work best when given direction from their superiors. When left to create this structure for themselves, they can have great difficulty.

### Facts, details and routine...

ISTJ employees are usually found in positions where they need to deal with a great amount of details. They have a hands-on approach to their work and take the time to organize and systematize everything with which they come into contact. Often, they are good at creating elaborate filing and index systems, allowing for easy retrieval of information. Others come to depend on them because ISTJs know exactly where everything is, or at least where everything should be.

They like working on projects that make sense to them. Great effort is put into their work in a thorough and careful way. They will continue working at it even though it means working beyond their regular day, rather than delegate to someone else who may not be able to do the work according to ISTJs' standards. They like to be in control of all aspects of the work they are doing.

ISTJs prefer to have meetings run in an orderly and specific manner with a precise agenda and schedule. They become irritated when too much time is spent processing information or dealing with interpersonal necessities.

### Follow rules and procedures...

# WORK STYLE OF THE ISTJ

ISTJs are good at giving clear, concise directions that are easy to follow because of their step-by-step format. They have a very linear approach to performing all tasks and are able to articulate this to others. They have a strict set of rules for doing all they do, and they need this structure to be effective. This procedural approach to everything, including interpersonal relationships at work, provides them with very tangible and specific ways of handling all kinds of situations. This means that if they are expected to be more personal or personable while at work, they will add this to their routine. They will factor in what to say, who to say it to, and how much time they should allot to doing it, until it becomes a part of their structure.

The ISTJs unwritten rulebook contains a long list of "shoulds" and "should nots" that they follow and demand others follow as well. They have difficulty trusting that people may be able to achieve an objective in their own way. They want to check in constantly and monitor progress more often than most people can tolerate.

They tend to expect others to work the same way they do. However, because ISTJs are extremely specific and accurate in all they do, they set unrealistic expectations that others may not be able to attain. This can frustrate their peers and get in the way of developing relationships at work.

## Can struggle with change...

Asking ISTJs to make changes can be challenging as it creates uncertainty for them. If someone up the chain of command asks them to change their approach to something they are working on or to make a procedural change, ISTJs usually respond with opposition. This is actually a tactic to buy time to think about what they are being asked to do. Ultimately, ISTJs will do what they believe their manager wants them to do, even if they are not in agreement. When in leadership positions, ISTJs expect to be obeyed and are prone to be strict disciplinarians to gain compliance.

# WORK STYLE OF THE ISTJ

Because they are so security oriented, ISTJs may uphold a procedure because it's always the way it's been done. They hold on to it long after it has outlived its usefulness. They have difficulty seeing the need for change and can be unresponsive and even argumentative when it is imposed on them.

Because ISTJs dislike the way change makes them feel, they appear inflexible and negative when it's introduced. They get their sense of security from maintaining and adhering to the tried and tested. Their preference is to not learn something new if they have already mastered the old. If a change is necessary, ISTJs will receive the information better if it is presented in terms of its concrete usefulness and the features and benefits of the change.

## Have difficulty seeing the big picture...

ISTJs run the risk of being so task-oriented they sometimes miss the more global picture of what is going on. There are things they cannot take a structured or ordered approach to, such as interpersonal dynamics or an unstable marketplace. It is very stressful for them to have to be involved with too much strategic planning, as they feel they are wasting time and not taking care of today's business. They tend to argue that, if no one is focusing on what is needed today, there will be no future for the company tomorrow.

ISTJs can easily be blind-sided, as they are so involved with their tasks they do not pay attention to what is going on around them. Often, they feel they are the last to know when told about something going on in the office, or they may be shocked to learn the company is restructuring or downsizing when everyone else has been reading the signals for a long time.

When presented with a new idea or concept, ISTJs will always demand proof and ask for very specific details. This can be extremely difficult, particularly for intuitive types who have not yet fleshed out all of the specifics of their ideas. ISTJs need to understand the

# Work Style of the ISTJ

demotivating impact this demand of proof has on others, and should learn to moderate their need for detail in situations where they might do better focusing on the bigger picture.

## Minimal social needs in the workplace...

ISTJs have a very minimal need for interpersonal interactions. They tend to have relationships that are defined by their roles at work. This can create tension and discomfort for other types with higher relational needs. ISTJs have difficulty understanding the value other people place on socializing. They consider it to be a waste of time.

They approach meeting their goals and objectives in a very specific and no-nonsense fashion. This can lead others to perceive them as being overly controlling or uncaring. It is not that they don't care. They find it difficult and awkward to express their feelings or appreciation to others at work. ISTJs often do not feel the need to praise others or even show professional or personal interest in them.

## Prefer behavioral conformity...

It may be very difficult for ISTJs to understand and respond to the needs of others when these are not the same as their own. This can lead them to discount or even discredit the other person. By learning to recognize the needs and values of others, they add a wider and more versatile perspective to their scope of experience and increase their ability to manage interpersonal relationships within the organization.

ISTJs may overlook those individuals who take small steps toward goals or performance improvements and reward only those whom they perceive to be star performers. ISTJs need encouragement and coaching to learn to give praise to those who are not as visibly productive as they are.

## Have difficulty setting limits or saying "no"...

# Work Style of the ISTJ

Because they are so dedicated in their approach and commitment to work, others tend to expect this high level of output without giving them adequate acknowledgement and appreciation. ISTJs are prone to periods of burnout and depression because they tend to carry such a large workload with little acknowledgement.

ISTJs often have difficulty delegating due to their extremely high standards. They need to have a great deal of confidence in someone before they will do so. This, and their difficulty saying no, also leads to overload and burnout.

## Work environment matters...

In general, ISTJs work to their full capacity to the benefit of everyone, if the following criteria or conditions are in place. The work

- requires them to use their ability to work with facts and details.

- is technical in nature.

- provides a certain amount of autonomy with significant amounts of time to work alone.

- lets them use their powers of concentration to complete their tasks and goals with minimal interruptions.

- involves a real or tangible product or service in an ordered, logical, and sequential manner.

- allows them to establish their goals and work toward them with necessary and sufficient resources.

- provides a well-defined organizational structure with clear and straightforward objectives that are not subject to unnecessary change.

## Work Style of the ISTJ

- environment is traditional in nature, and they are not expected to take unnecessary risks or use untested methods or experimental approaches to their work.

- provides them with the opportunity to achieve and take on increasing levels of responsibility.

- has a minimal expectation for social interaction and politics.

- provides objective criticism for evaluating performance, and the ISTJs are evaluated and appreciated for meeting the requirements of their job description.

- has tangible and measurable goals, and it rewards them for their practical approach to their work.

- allows them enough time to prepare their work, and does not require excessive teamwork where ISTJs are expected to work too closely with a group.

# Work Style of the ISTJ

## Team Contributions

A team is an integral part of any organization. It consists of a group of two or more people working together to achieve a specific task or outcome. More than ever, team members need to work together effectively to accomplish tasks. As many teams are now cross-functional and self-directed, with no one person having direct authority over others, it is important to recognize the unique contributions each type makes to a team.

By understanding the different approaches, strengths, and weaknesses of each type, the organization can maximize a team's diversity by matching specific tasks with the team members who are most suited to them, based on their type preference. An understanding of types can help individuals see how different perspectives can enhance brainstorming, problem solving, and conflict resolution. It can also help with team selection to ensure teams are not too one-sided and, as a result, overlook aspects of problems other types would have seen and addressed.

## ISTJ Team Contributions

ISTJs contribute to their team by providing reality-based organizational skills to get things done with minimum fanfare. ISTJs go about organizing and maintaining structure and format, ensuring that every little detail is taken care of so that, in the end, the team will achieve its objectives. They like to know what is expected of them and the roles and responsibilities of others prior to setting out to do a group task. This allows them to hold themselves and others accountable for each step of the group process, whether it is their role or not.

# Work Style of the ISTJ

ISTJs' primary contribution to the team is providing hard-working, efficient effort to get the task done on time. Their common-sense approach to problem solving helps the team stay focused and on-track. ISTJs are highly organized and like the team to run in a structured, efficient manner.

Because of their attention to facts and detail, ISTJs can influence the direction of the team by using logical arguments backed by specifics and realism. They are also open to listening to facts presented by others and will spend time clarifying tasks, methods, and expectations. Unfortunately, ISTJs, like other people with a preference for introversion, may withhold information. They expect everyone to honour their commitments and are impatient with those who lack follow-through and do not comply with the agreed upon timelines of the team.

Other team members can view ISTJs as far too serious and taking the fun out of the team process by insisting that everyone stays tightly to the agenda and expecting them not to bring personal issues into the discussion. ISTJs tend to focus so much on task and detail they lose sight of the bigger picture and why the team is working together in the first place. They can become more effective on teams when they develop interpersonal communication skills and learn to have more fun while in the pursuit of the team's objectives.

ISTJs do not like to waste time and can become irritated by team members who do this by discussing personal or unrelated subjects. They prefer people to get to the point and may appear disapproving when there is too much time spent talking about personal and unrelated subjects.

# Work Style of the ISTJ

## Leadership Style

This section provides information on how individuals of this personality type, in their leadership roles, determine what needs to be done and how they create the circumstances for achieving the desired outcomes.

All leaders have individual preferences for exercising power or control, task orientation, relationship needs, and the demonstration of principles and values. These vary in intensity in each type and in the way they are demonstrated in the role of leader. The following reflects the characteristics of the leadership style of the ISTJ.

## The ISTJ Leader

ISTJs are often found in leadership roles because of their decisive and authoritarian leadership style. They have enormous respect for rules, regulations, and preserving the status quo. Employees always know where they stand with ISTJ leaders because ISTJs tend to do everything by the book. They also expect everyone to follow rules and procedures without question or exception.

The ISTJ's temperament is traditionalist. They work hard and long to preserve and conserve tradition. As they require a sense of belonging and stability, they will work to create this if it is not already there. To ISTJ leaders, tradition and stability go hand-in-hand. They appreciate the value of rituals, anniversaries, and celebrations, and will ensure these are part of the normal course of events within the company.

ISTJ leaders work effectively within hierarchies that are well laid out, with consistent, straightforward policies and procedures. Their excellence in managing processes makes them naturals in all kinds of organizations. Meeting deadlines and budgets, and ensuring productivity and accountability are strengths of ISTJs. They use the same approach in managing people, equipment, and processes.

## Hard work, task and goal oriented...

ISTJs do not always seek out management positions, yet tend to find themselves in these positions because ISTJs are so reliable and hard-working. Unfortunately, this does not mean they are inspirational leaders. Their natural tendency is to drive people toward the completion of tasks the same way they drive themselves.

Because of their need for security, ISTJ leaders want their subordinates to work in a consistent and predictable fashion. They have difficulty when people do not follow a subscribed routine and may judge this negatively rather than trying to understand it. ISTJs become more effective leaders when they learn to trust the flow of other people's work styles, thereby reducing the stress that comes when they feel the need to "police" their staff.

ISTJ leaders usually reward those workers who abide by the rules and get their jobs done with minimal supervision. Their idea of a perfect employee is someone who is much like them. This can lead them to hire others of the same type who fit in easily but may cause the organization to lack versatility. Often ISTJ leaders can be driven to meet their deadlines, so much so that they are oblivious to the impact it is having on people. Their desire for efficiency can demotivate employees and take away all sense of personal satisfaction. At worst, the workplace can become rigid and excessively demanding, creating high absenteeism, hostility, and stress.

ISTJs are more comfortable providing their employees with structure and direction than positive feedback and appreciation. They tend to believe people should earn appreciation, and they withhold it from those who fall short of performance expectations.

# WORK STYLE OF THE ISTJ

## Functional, not fun or feeling...

ISTJ leaders are oriented toward following procedures to achieve their goals. They usually give feedback to get people back on course and to correct deviations from the established norm. Sometimes this feedback is perceived as negative criticism rather than valuable feedback.

Because of their task orientation, ISTJs often have difficulty with the relational side of management. They don understand other types who have different needs and motivations. They believe everyone should have a similar task orientation. ISTJs are at a loss as to how to get these people to adopt an attitude like their own. They don't easily accept these differences or think of them as normal rather than aberrant behaviours.

Another drawback of ISTJ leaders is they can create an environment that is so functional and conservative they take all the fun out of it employees of other types. Even having creature comforts such as a comfortable chair or well-equipped staff kitchen can be judged by ISTJs to be a waste of money. If not effectively brought to their attention, ISTJs' efficient nature tends to quickly diminish and demotivate employees.

## Formal and conservative...

As leaders, ISTJs often adopt the style of mentors or former leaders whose style achieved results. When they have not had a model to follow, ISTJ leaders will set their own standards that they expect themselves and others to follow. They don't try to be like themselves, they strive to achieve excellent performance of the role of leader.

ISTJ leaders are conservative and consistent, and can be counted on to do the right thing at the right time. They will put out extra effort when they see a precise need to get things done. However, they must buy into something before they can move ahead. They will not initiate

# Work Style of the ISTJ

change for its own sake, or be open to suggestions from subordinates as to a better or different way of doing things. ISTJs can even have difficulty seeing why someone might want to do things differently. However, once convinced of the merit of the change, they will support it and adjust themselves accordingly.

ISTJs tend to be very predictable. They manage in a very formal manner and are exceptionally loyal to the organization. They are far more oriented to tasks than relationships, and quite often the people with whom they work feel far less important than the job at hand. Although ISTJ managers do not set about to make people feel this way, those who have higher relationship needs can be demotivated by their behaviour.

# Work Style of the ISTJ

## *Stress and Self-Protective Behavior*

This next section talks about how the ISTJ behaves when they are not at their best, or when put on the defensive. In typology, these are referred to as the "least preferred" or "inferior functions."

During the development of the personality, it is normal and predictable that we first develop our most preferred functions. However, other functions don't always get developed as they are harder to use and used less frequently. When we have to use other functions that don't come as easy to us, it is challenging and takes more energy. We tend to act more from our emotions than from our developed self.

Each type has the potential to overuse or abuse its preferences. This is likely to happen when individuals are under stress or pressure or they feel threatened in some way. They will behave differently than usual.

The following paragraphs describe some of the ways this occurs with the ISTJ.

### Withdraws and does not communicate...

ISTJs are intensely private people who are not usually forthcoming with how they feel, and consider these emotions to be unimportant. They are equally ill at ease when forced to deal with the emotions of others and tend to withdraw even further into themselves when faced with a situation that calls for a response to emotions.

This low need for emotional expression and high need for privacy can cause others around them to have difficulty understanding ISTJs. Their lack of emotional availability and their uncommunicative stance can sometimes create very serious interpersonal problems in the workplace.

# Work Style of the ISTJ

Because they are uncomfortable dealing with feelings, ISTJs tend to avoid their own as well. They may not even be aware of the aura of disapproval or impatience they are projecting. This lack of clarity in their communication leaves others feeling frustrated, defensive, and reluctant to approach them.

## Catastrophizes...

Intuition is the least developed function of ISTJs. Because of this, they are unable to use it to generate positive possibilities, instead conjuring up one worst-case scenario after another. When caught up in their self-protective system, they can't think of anything positive, imagining the very worst that ever happened to anyone. Even the thought of doing something different can provoke horrific imaginings. The world becomes an anxiety-producing and threatening place with a dismal future ahead.

Because their imaginings are thought of as facts by the ISTJ, they become increasingly paranoid about doing anything new or different. Just thinking about it can cause them to become overwhelmed, irritable, and resistant to anything they are told to the contrary. Even in the case where the present circumstances are causing the problem, the won't change. As their fear of the unknown has triggered this response, ISTJs imagine the current stressful situation will continue into the future, as will their inability to handle it effectively.

At worst, when ISTJs are unable to face feelings that arise from their fear of the unknown, they may resort to some type of addiction, either to work, controlling others, or substance abuse to establish a sense of control in their world. To make matters worse, they might even come up with unrealistic plans for solving their problems and then must deal with their disappointment when they fail to achieve results.

Without a clear-cut plan for approaching the future, ISTJs leave themselves at risk of relying too heavily on the traditional way things have always been done and not addressing the reality of a changing

## Work Style of the ISTJ

world or marketplace. They are prone to overlooking the long-range impact of change in favour of their day-to-day reality.

### Loses control over facts and details...

When the intuitive function has been developed sufficiently, people are comfortable with generalizing and suggesting ideas and theories without first having to flesh out all the facts and details. They can address the specifics at a later date. When ISTJs are in their self-protective system, any generalization is a threat, as is any inaccuracy or possibility. They refuse to move from their position.

ISTJs are most comfortable dealing with practical realities, finding safety and security in this very tangible world. When excessively stressed or fatigued, ISTJs are unable to maintain their firm grasp on detail and begin to have uncharacteristic difficulty being objective, specific, and analytical. They feel out of control and unable to be rational about what is happening to them. Often unable to draw logical conclusions about what is going on with themselves, they sometimes distort facts or simply become unsure of things that are normally second nature to them.

### Behave impulsively...

During stress, ISTJs become impulsive and thoughtless, only later judging themselves as having been irresponsible and reckless. Spontaneity shows itself as snappy orders or hurtful comments, and they fly off the handle with an uncharacteristic lack of control over what they are saying. It's hard to see that the ISTJs anxiety, confusion, and uncertainty is causing their reaction. Others are surprised and feel blindsided by the ISTJs' impulsive reactions.

It's as though the filter they had has come off and ISTJs let everything that has built up inside of them related to work, people, or anything else that has happened to them out, whether it is related to the issue or not. Their response is way out of proportion to the event at hand which caused this eruption.

The dependable and stable ISTJs tend to be fascinated by others with compulsive and irresponsible behaviours. ISTJs may actually marry alcoholics or be attracted to people they are somehow disfunctional so they can rescue or reform them.

## Become rigid and demand conformity...

In their desire to maintain structure and uniformity, ISTJs run the risk of becoming rigid and inflexible. They tend to overuse rules and regulations to control behaviour, and reject the contributions of others without adequate reflection. They can become so bound to precision and detail, they ignore the bigger picture and the feelings of those involved in favour of interpreting the exact letter of the law.

The obsessiveness ISTJs show when caught up in their intuitive function responses can repel others who would normally try to help them. They will often alienate people through their scepticism, causing others to take an even more rigid and defensive stance. They may even begin to believe the only ones capable of doing the work right are themselves. This can lead them to work even more compulsively, spending long and lonely hours doing everything, or doing the same thing over and over again until they do it right – to their standard of perfection. ISTJs are often the poster people for workaholics and are quite capable of damaging themselves.

## Approaches people impersonally...

ISTJs can be so task-oriented they may be oblivious to the impact they have on others. Sometimes they overlook interpersonal relationship needs because of their extreme task orientation. While ISTJs often feel positive and warm towards people, they fail to verbalize these feelings and therefore leave people in the dark as to what they are feeling. They tend to rely heavily on written

## Work Style of the ISTJ

communication rather than face-to-face contact, as it allows them to control and organize the flow of their thoughts.

ISTJs feel secure when everyone around them is logical and unemotional. They tentatively approach most situations that call for them to express appreciation or gratitude, as they are frightened of losing control. Interpersonal interactions cause them a great deal of anxiety, since there is no prescribed outcome. They try not to get involved in personal relationships on the job for fear of where it might lead. Very easily, they may be seen as insensitive or harsh because they often use judgement rather than empathy in their responses to others. They can easily steamroll less assertive people when demanding everyone conform to their way of doing things.

# Work Style of the ISTJ

## Pressing the ISTJs Buttons

The following are things that can cause ISTJs to shift to their self-protective system where they behave in an emotionally driven or reaction fashion.

- Anything new that presents itself – a previously inexperienced event, changes in plans – any of these are likely to evoke all of the negative possibilities of what might go wrong. Whatever has no basis in past experience is suspect, and will generate anxiety and worry.

- Periods of prolonged stress, conflict, or ongoing change are a trigger for the highly responsible ISTJ. Losing their task focus, they engage is harsh, sarcastic or catastrophizing dialogue about what might happen.

- Too much time spent in extraverted activities. They may become somewhat scattered and make decisions based on too little information. When confronted with this fact, they may stubborn refuse to reconsider their premature decisions.

- Spending too much time alone leaves them prone to replaying memories in an unproductive manner. This further triggers them into playing out negative future possibilities and becoming lost in this inner reality. Spending excessive time focusing on details may also trigger an undeveloped function response.

- Taking on too much responsibility and hard work without receiving appreciation for too long. When they feel taken for granted, they may erupt with an emotional explosion and say things they didn't even know they felt. This can cause them acute embarrassment once balance has been restored.

## WORK STYLE OF THE ISTJ

- With their high need for accountability, they can be easily triggered if deadlines are not honoured, or new ideas are introduced into a pre-existing plan without sufficient notice for them. Even simple things such as a topic being introduced five minutes before a meeting should end can be enough to spark a response.

- Taking on too much responsibility and hard work without receiving appreciation for too long. When they feel taken for granted, they may erupt with an emotional explosion and say things they didn't even know they felt. This can cause them acute embarrassment once balance has been restored.

- Being expected to follow or have faith in someone of whom they have no previous experience. If other types have the ability to take risks, ISTJs can quickly judge them to be foolhardy, irresponsible, and immature.

- If a project goes too far off schedule, ISTJs may uncharacteristically blame others or the environment. They may feel sorry for themselves and indulge in self-pity.

- Someone else's desire to make a change or take a risk. Whether a work superior, partner, spouse, or child, they will often respond with a barrage of negative possibilities, causing the other person to feel a lack of support and a need to withdraw from the ISTJ.

# WORK STYLE OF THE ISTJ

## Shifting from Self-Protective Behavior

The following are ways that ISTJs have found to reduce stress and regain balance in day-to-day functioning.

- By asking for more information or details, especially when they are being introduced to new situations. It also is helpful for them to go into new situations asking for this information up front.

- Spending time to themselves to reflect on how new situations are relative to, and connected with, past experiences. Once they make these connections and put the situation into perspective, they are more able to pursue new activities. By developing alternative plans and focusing on specific details, they can reduce their usual undeveloped function response.

- By asking for the assistance of trusted friends or colleagues to help them modify their perspectives. This can help them to begin to control their anxious ruminations and worrying through the use of objective analysis and feedback.

- It is extremely important to ISTJs at such times that others take them seriously, so being able to unstress and vent with an objective and impartial listener who does not offer advice or solutions until it is solicited, is extremely helpful.

- Having someone take over some of the overwhelming details that have contributed to the ISTJ's stress and fatigue when they have taken on too much work, without making the ISTJ feel like a failure for not being able to do it without help.

- To be reminded during an episode of their undeveloped function that their worrying is a predictable and normal part of their personality type.

# Work Style of the ISTJ

- Taking time out to listen to poetry, music, or anything to do with the arts helps ISTJs engage the undeveloped function in a positive way. Often ISTJs' choice of artists tends toward the expressive, romantic, and dramatic, which is the opposite of their personality.

- Physical activity that brings the ISTJ back into the here and now, and this shift out of the undeveloped function can open the way for the resolution of whatever has triggered their stress.

- Activities that engage their sensory awareness without seeming too irresponsible to them will also help reduce their stress and tension. Although these are simple activities, they are often quite difficult for ISTJs to do yet imperative to their psychological balance.

- Reading or watching science fiction stories or movies, or allowing themselves to indulge in fantasy or daydreams also helps ISTJs restore equilibrium.

- Allow their negative fantasies to play out to completion before they pull themselves back into reality. To them, it might feel as though they are being swept up into a vortex, but to resist it only leads to further exhaustion. The most natural pathway out of their undeveloped function response is through their Thinking function, which provides them with the factual information about what is real. At this point, they can take back control and know that things are going to work out well.

- Use their ability to utilize details to help them out of an undeveloped function response. This will stop them from focusing on what is not working and imagining negative possibilities. This will also prevent them from getting stuck in a rut and imagining the future in dismal, pessimistic terms.

# WORK STYLE OF THE ISTJ

- Involvement in the predictive sciences, such as astrology sciences, relying on the credibility of these systems through the detailed eyewitness testimony over long periods of time. They can use this type of information to assist them in controlling their negative outlook toward an imagined, insecure, or unsafe future. It provides them with a way of becoming more familiar with their intuition so they are not so frightened when it is activated.

- Through experiencing undeveloped function responses and working through them, ISTJs can begin to develop more of a tolerance for the unknown. It helps them to stand back from their abundant responsibilities and re-evaluate what is truly important to them. This usually involves making their family and relationships a higher priority.

- Using their Thinking function to lead them out of their subjective reactions to their sensory overload. They can create a task-specific plan to provide order to the chaos of detail that has overwhelmed them.

# Work Style of the ISTJ

## *Bibliography*

Barr, L. and Barr, N. (1989) **THE LEADERSHIP EQUATION**: Leadership, Management and the Myers-Briggs. Austin, Texas: Eakin Press.

Barr, L. and Barr, N. (1994) **LEADERSHIP DEVELOPMENT**: Maturity and Power. Austin, Texas: Eakin Press.

Bridges, William. (1992) **THE CHARACTER OF ORGANIZATIONS**: Using Jungian Type in Organizational Development. Palo Alto, California: Davies-Black Publishing.

Brownsword, Alan W. (1988) **PSYCHOLOGICAL TYPE**: An Introduction. San Anselmo, California: The Human Resources Management, Inc.

Isachsen, Olaf and Berens, Linda V. (1988) **WORKING TOGETHER**: A Personality-Centered Approach to Management. San Juan Capistrano, California: Institute for Management Development.

Isachsen, Olaf. (1996) **JOINING THE ENTREPRENEURIAL ELITE.** Palo Alto, California: Davies-Black Publishing.

Keirsey, David and Bates, Marilyn. (1984) **PLEASE UNDERSTAND ME**: Character and Temperament Types. Del Mar, California: Prometheus Nemesis Book Co.

Keirsey, David. (1991) **PORTRAITS OF TEMPERAMENT**. Del Mar, California: Prometheus Nemesis Book Co.

Kroeger, Otto and Thuesen, Janet M. (1992) **TYPE TALK AT WORK**: How the 16 Personality Types Determine Your Success on the Job. New York, NY: Dell Publishing.

# Work Style of the ISTJ

McCaulley, Mary H. (1989) **THE MYERS-BRIGGS TYPE INDICATOR AND LEADERSHIP**. Gainesville, Florida: Center for Applications of Psychological Type, Inc.

Myers, Katharine D. and Kirby, Linda K. (1994) **INTRODUCTION TO TYPE**: Dynamics and Development, Exploring the Next Level of Type. Palo Alto, California: Consulting Psychologists Press, Inc.

Myers, Isabel Briggs and McCaulley, Mary H. (1986) **MANUAL:** A Guide to the Development and Use of the Myers-Briggs Type Indicator. Palo Alto, California: Consulting Psychologists Press, Inc.

Myers, Isabel Briggs, and Myers, Peter B. (1995) **GIFTS DIFFERING**: Understanding Personality Types. Palo Alto, California: Davies-Black Publishing.

Provost, Judith A. (1990) **WORK, PLAY AND TYPE**: Achieving Balance in Your Life. Palo Alto, California: Davies-Black Publishing.

# WORK STYLE OF THE ISTJ

## About the Author

## Anne Dranitsaris, Ph.D.

### Behavioral Change Expert, Executive & Leadership Coach, Author

Anne Dranitsaris is the founder and creator of the Striving Styles™ Personality System, a neuropsychological approach to achieving potential that blends personality type, needs theory and the latest advances in neuroscience. Anne uses the Striving Styles in her work with individuals, couples, parents and leaders in organizations. She has more than 35 years experience working in private practice and with leaders and teams in organizations. She helps clients develop emotional intelligence, behavioural competence, and relationship skills. She also provides business relationship coaching for individuals experiencing difficulties with their business because of conflict in primary relationships (partners, leadership groups, teams, boards, etc.).

### Committed to Life –Long Learning

Anne has her doctorate in philosophy from the Open International University for Complementary Medicine (WHO). She completed her psychotherapy training at the Centre for Training in Psychotherapy (Toronto) and studied at the Masterson Institute for Disorders of the Self (New York). She is also a graduate of the International School for Spiritual Sciences (Montreal). Anne attended Ryerson University and the Institute for Management Training for organizational development and management studies. She has also completed postgraduate programs in Cognitive Behavioural Therapy, Spiritual Self-Schema Development, and Alternate Dispute Resolution (Stitt, Feld, Handy). She received her certificate from the University of Toronto, Faculty of Social Work for Mindfulness-Based Stress Reduction Professional Training. Neuro Linguistic Programming (NLP), Hypnotherapy, Emotional Intelligence (EQ-i). Recently she completed three online programs with the National Institute for the

# Work Style of the ISTJ

Clinical Application of Behavioral Medicine (New Brain Science, Trauma & Clinical Applications of Mindfulness).

## Clinical Practice

Anne works with individuals, couples and families for the treatment of eating disorders and addiction, depression, anxiety, stress and anger management, and relationship and family conflicts to name a few. She offers both brief, intense psychotherapy and long-term psychotherapy using a wide range of treatment methodologies she has incorporated over the years. Using brain-based and mindfulness approaches, Anne helps people understand their personality, needs and emotions leading to changes in dysfunctional patterns of behaviour, thinking or emotions. She also provides ADD, ADHD & Family Counselling to help parents of children who are having difficulty dealing with the behaviors of their child.

As a psychotherapist, Anne draws from a number of schools of theory and practical disciplines, including Cognitive-Behavioral Therapy, Psychodynamic Therapy, Self-Psychology, Mindfulness, Acceptance and Commitment Therapy. Incorporating her experience with these methodologies, she is able to approach each individual from a holistic, psycho-educational perspective. Her therapeutic approach includes looking at thoughts, feelings, beliefs and behaviors; finding patterns of behaviour that are limiting to the individual and providing tools for developing greater insight and awareness, and for changing and adapting to new behaviours.

## Consulting Practice

Anne became one of Toronto's first Executive Coaches in the late 1980's. She could see the direct application of the therapeutic tools to the corporate world, which drove her to expand her work into that realm. Anne began using the title of Corporate Therapist to indicate the depth with which she worked with leaders and teams developing emotional intelligence, behavioral competence and relationship skills in organizations. She has also used her unique approach to work through dysfunctional relationships, partnerships, teams and boards.

# Work Style of the ISTJ

She has also worked with several international organizations which used a matrix organizational structure to help them understand the cultural dynamics and behavior of the various countries involved to improve overall performance. Her corporate therapy and behavioural consulting approach includes assessing, educating, training and coaching to develop greater self-awareness, awareness of others, improved team dynamics and overall corporate functioning.

## Successful Entrepreneur

Before devoting herself to the development of the Striving Styles and the publishing of Who Are You Meant to Be? Earlier in her career, Anne was the owner of several successful clinics (Annex Natural Health Clinic, Dranitsaris Psychotherapy Services, and Centre for Mindful Therapies). Her first consulting business was Sage Developmental Resources which her daughter, Heather Hilliard, grew into Caliber Leadership System. She also played a critical role in the start up of two businesses, Figure & Face as Clinical Director and Seroyal International as Director of Development. She is now partner at Sage Kahuna Enterprises, using a business model of few employees and many contract specialists. Anne has experience running businesses of a few to up to 50 employees as well as consulting to those who benefit from her expertise.

## Author & Published Writer

Anne is also a frequently published writer and speaker on a broad range of topics on organizational dysfunction, behaviour, emotional intelligence and personality styles and their impact in the workplace. She has also been published and quoted in such publications as O, The Oprah Magazine, Chatelaine, Canadian Living, hrprofessional, TrainingIndustry.com, Organizational Development Network and earlier this year in the British HR Magazine. Her writing is both insightful and easy to understand, giving readers what they need to deal with the challenges they face at work and in life.

During the past 20 years, Anne has authored more than 100 reports for the Striving Styles and the Myers-Briggs Type Indicator including

## WORK STYLE OF THE ISTJ

the Behavioural Interview Guide. She also wrote Jung's Typology for the Workplace Series, 3 distinct reports for Leaders, Teams and Employees. In 2013, Who Are You Meant to Be? A ground-breaking step-by-step process for discovering and achieving your true potential was published by Sourcebooks. This work is the culmination of her work with typology in a clinical and organizational setting. She has also written NOW Fix Your Relationship and is currently completing her most recent work, Stop Being at the Mercy of Your Codependent Brain.

# Work Style of the ISTJ

## MBTI & Striving Styles Services

We provide the following services in conjunction with the Striving Styles Personality System or the Myers-Briggs Type Indicator (MBTI) personality assessment instruments:

### Testing and Interpretation

Determine personality type to identify strengths, unique abilities, and developmental needs. Gain insight into the different communication and work styles to learn how to capitalize quickly on strengths and work to communicate as effectively as possible, while acknowledging and respecting differences.

### Interpretive Reporting

Based on personality type Testing and Interpretation information (above), provide individualized reports which can be used for determining leadership profiles, role suitability, compliment current hiring practices; provide comparative profiles to identify potential strengths and challenges in working relationships (e.g. manager/employee, manager/manager, employee/employee).

### Team Profiles

Based on personality type Testing and Interpretation information (above), providing detailed composite information for Teams, including overall team trends, strengths, blind spots, and unique contributions of individual team members. Creating highly functioning teams by utilizing individual skills and abilities, and by improving communication, conflict resolution and problem solving.

### Selection Candidate Assessments

Based on personality type Testing and Interpretation information (above), comprehensive reports to determine role suitability in the hiring process, with comparison section to potential managers or team members (as required) to determine areas of similarity and difference, complimentary skills or conflict.

### Training
Conduct programs for employee development that can be tailored to meet an organization's specific needs, including introductory and advanced programs, team building, communication training, Type, Temperament, and Conflict Styles. Training can be conducted in workshop or module format or within the context of a team building or strategic planning session.

### Leadership and Employee Development Programs
Implement programs to develop leadership and employee capabilities as well as support continuous learning to enhance organizational performance. Integrate personality assessment with performance management and employee development programs, selection and succession planning, competency-based development, and leadership development and training based on Jung typology.

### Organizational/Executive Team Profiles and Strategic Planning
Based on type Testing and Interpretation of information (above), creating a detailed composite report of the current executive team to create an organizational profile. Identify relative strengths and challenges of leadership team, including competency gaps. Conduct leadership training sessions to optimize team performance. Facilitate strategic planning based on organizational type, needs, goals, vision, values, etc.

### Critical Conflict Resolution
Intensive training sessions for teams in functional or relational crisis. Team training in personality type, including individual profiles. Systemic approach with specific focus on understanding individual differences, communication styles, conflict styles, relational and

# Work Style of the ISTJ

interaction style. Focus on understanding, cooperation and problem solving skills.

## Leadership Coaching

Provide one-on-one coaching to increase individual effectiveness using Jung Typology as a working model. Coaching leaders to develop based on self understanding and providing a very detailed understanding of what drives themselves and others with whom they interact. Specifically tailored coaching programs aligned with competency development to enhance individual strengths and improve overall work performance.

# Work Style of the ISTJ

## MBTI & Striving Styles Products

### Jung's Typology for the Workplace Series

### Book One: Understanding Employee Behaviour

This book provides a collection of insights into predictable behaviours for each of the types as well as what they need in order to be more successful at work. Individuals will better understand their work style, motivation and needs. Managers will get valuable information as to how to deal with the challenges of the type and employees will gain information about how they might adjust their behaviour at work.

### Book Two: Understanding Team Behaviour

This book offers insight into what role each personality type will assume on a team. It provides information on how they tend to use the team as a means to achieving their objectives at work or getting their social and emotional needs met. Each of the types has their own challenges when working with a team and the type of frustrations they are likely to experience when working with others. It offers guidance on how to maximize performance on the team.

### Book Three: Understanding Leader Behaviour

This book provides a collection of insights into predictable behaviours for each of the types as leaders. It demonstrates how the distinct styles of each type will organize their work and environment; manage the performance of their direct reports; and how their leadership style impacts others. It shows how leaders prefers to function in everyday working situations helps them build self awareness. Leaders will benefit from the framework typology offers for their own development.

### **Brain-Based Behavioral Interview Guide**

# WORK STYLE OF THE ISTJ

How an individual behaves in the workplace is greatly influenced by their Personality Type. Behavioural interviewing is a structured interviewing strategy built on the premise that past behaviour is the best predictor of future performance in similar circumstances. The behavioural interview questions help determine how the candidate has utilized his/her natural strengths, worked at developing their lesser-preferred functions and whether they recognize their work and leadership styles. Using a brain-based approach to behavioural interviewing goes a long way to minimizing risk in the hiring process and helps you to build a successful onboarding strategy based on the needs of the candidate.

With 185 pages, this extensive resource guide includes:
- description of each of the 16 Types (Jung, MBTI) or Striving Style Squads
- information on best work environment, work style, satisfiers and dissatisfiers
- description of the key behavioural challenges for each Type
- behavioural questions for each of these challenges for each Type
- extensive variety of behaviour-based questions to choose from
- directory of all the behavioural interview questions for each area of challenge

## Who Are You Meant to Be?
A ground-breaking Step-by-Step Process for Discovering and Fulfilling Your True Potential by Anne Dranitsaris, Ph.D. & Heather Dranitsaris Hilliard (Sourcebooks, Inc. 2013) Available on Amazon.ca or Amazon.com

## Striving Styles Personality System Reports
All reports written by Anne Dranitsaris, Heather Dranitsaris-Hilliard & Nancy Dranitsaris

## Individual Reports (Approx. 40 pages) to be used with the SSPS:

# Work Style of the ISTJ

General Reports
Leadership Reports (8)
Relationship Reports (8)
Work Style Reports (8)
Career Reports (8)
Leveraging Your Squad (16)

## Myers-Briggs Type Indicator Reports

All reports written by Anne Dranitsaris, Heather Dranitsaris-Hilliard & Nancy Dranitsaris

## Individual Reports (Approx. 40 pages) to be used with the MBTI:

Brain-based Leadership Reports (16)
Brain-based Career Reports (16)
Brain-based Relationship Reports (16)

## White Papers

The Next Evolution of Jung's Typology and the Myers-Briggs Type Indicator® by Anne Dranitsaris & Heather Dranitsaris-Hilliard

## For more information, contact:

## Anne Dranitsaris, Ph.D.

Caliber Leadership Systems
422 – 283 Danforth Ave
Toronto, ON  M4K 1Y2

Telephone: 416.406.3939
Email: AnneD@annedranitsaris.com
www.AnneDranitsaris.com
www.caliberleadershipcoaching.com
www.StrivingStyles.com

Made in the USA
Columbia, SC
17 December 2019